DO THE BASICS

Better

A SALES GUIDE

FOR THE SMALL BUSINESS OWNER

JOSE "JOE" MIR

ISBN: 979-8-35090-717-9

"Champions are brilliant at the basics." ~ John Wooden

FOREWORD

LET'S FACE IT, MOST PEOPLE DISLIKE SELLING and have a negative perception of the sales process and the chatty, "pushy" people who do it for a living. It's no coincidence it takes a very special person to serve in this role. And serve well. And serve *consistently* well.

So, it's no coincidence that many business owners shy away from this activity even though it may be one of the most important keys to building their businesses. "Build it and they will come" may work in the movie theater but not necessarily in the real world.

According to the U.S. Small Business Administration [SBA], less than 40% of small business owners have college degrees. And it's safe to assume the percentage of those who graduated college and later attended a basic sales training course is even smaller! Having said that, I do not believe a college degree is required to start and/or build a successful business. There are plenty of examples of people who never earned a post-graduate degree – Steve Jobs, Mark Zuckerberg, Bill Gates, Anna Wintour, Richard Branson, Debbi Fields, Ralph Lauren, Henry Ford ... shall I go on?

You get the point.

Degree or no degree, I *do* believe all business owners – regardless of educational background -- can benefit from a basic guide to increasing sales.

SO WHAT MAKES ME SUCH AN EXPERT, YOU ASK ...
My goal in this handbook is to provide you, the ambitious small business owner, with **BENCHMARK PRACTICES** taught to me during my 30 years in the corporate selling world. I had the great fortune to attend, as well as

facilitate, some of the best sales training programs at Johnson & Johnson over a 25-year period.

Prior to Johnson & Johnson, I worked at Baxter International and Quaker Oats [now part of PepsiCo]. Both offered excellent sales training, as well. I was also fortunate to participate in many outside training courses facilitated by some of the best sales consultants in the country.

My sales experience goes from having less than $1 million in annual sales responsibility to $1 billion. That second one is a big number, trust me. I led sales teams at the national and international levels and closed many multi-million dollar deals. I earned numerous sales and sales management awards and [modesty aside for a moment, forgive me] was considered among the best at Johnson & Johnson. From a personal perspective, I consider my claim to fame to be recognition for my efforts in Latin America. It got me featured on the JNJ Annual Report. Not bad for a sales guy!

In addition to attending best in-class sales training that Johnson & Johnson had to offer, I was always curious and willing to sharpen my craft by reading some of the best sales and business books. As a sales professional, I was restless and always eager to find the best way to get the job done and be the best.

I distinctly remember reading my first sales book as a freshman at the University of Miami in Coral Gables, FL -- *The Greatest Salesman in the World* by the incomparable and timeless Og Mandino. That book remains on my shelf today, nearly 40 years later! Its timeless tenets are as powerful as they were four decades ago.

I have also managed some of the best and brightest salespeople in the country. Recruiting, developing and hiring top talent has always been a passion of mine. I was also fortunate to inherit some great sales representatives that taught me their tricks and tips. All this has given me the ability to immediately spot a great salesperson. Unfailingly, it starts with attitude, a desire to be the best, intellectual curiosity and an empathetic spirit.

So, there you have it. My credentials in a mere six paragraphs.

TIME TO PAY IT FORWARD …

What follows on these pages is a summary of what I consider **THE BEST OF MY LEARNINGS** from across my sales career. No fluff, just the good stuff! One or two laboratory sittings should be sufficient time to read this handbook. Like a great sales call, it doesn't have to be long, just on the mark.

I hope these insights provide you with many benefits, I truly do. I'm at that stage in life where the desire to help others really kicks in. Even if you take away a single pearl of wisdom or find only one "A-ha!" message, I promise you it will be well worth the price.

Let's do this!

TABLE OF CONTENTS

"If you don't have a competitive advantage, don't compete." – Jack Welch

CHAPTER 1

YOUR VALUE PROPOSITION

If we were sitting on a park bench somewhere on a sunny day – two complete strangers striking up a casual conversation – and I asked you what you did for a living, and you tell me you were in sales, you would tell me the name of your company and mention the type of product or service you peddle.

It would sound impressive, right?

"So, tell me, what's your companies or product's value proposition?" I ask.

Would you sit there with a blank look on your face for several seconds before mumbling something taken directly from the *Playbook of Overused Business Buzzwords?*

Or would you spend the next 15 seconds clearly articulating why there's a need for your product, how your product fills that need in a way no other product can, how your product is changing the world for the better, and at a price point your target will accept?

I hope you'd bowl me over with your clarity and eloquence. But probably not if you're like so many other sales people out there today.

What's your company's and/or your product's Value Proposition?
Let's start with a few simple questions:

- *If your company or product did not exist, what would be different?*

- *Would your customers care?*

- *Would their financial positions or lives be impacted?*

- *Would your customers' customers suffer in any way?*

Hopefully, things *would* be quite different, they *would* care, and it *would* affect their ability to serve their customers in a meaningful way. That would validate the need for your product and the opportunity to meet that need, improve the lives of your customers and their customers, and everyone walks away better for the experience.

That's why you must be very clear about your unique Value Proposition.

In my three decades in Corporate America with three *Fortune 500* companies, I have seen countless, carefully crafted Value Propositions ... and many didn't cut the mustard. Some were so grandiose and self-serving, they were outright comical!

A truly *great* Value Proposition is one that allows your company and/or product to clearly differentiate itself from your competitors. It cuts to the chase and leaves zero ambiguity.

Every year for as long as America has existed, so many well-meaning, ambitious business people start out wanting to launch a great new product or company ... but most fail. In many cases, it's because they failed to take the time to craft a Value Proposition.

In his book *Good to Great: Why Some Companies Make the Leap ... and Others Don't*, author Jim Collins talks about the curiously named *Hedgehog Concept*. An ancient Greek parable states, "The fox knows many things, but the hedgehog knows one big thing." In the parable, the sly and clever fox uses many strategies to try and catch the hedgehog. It lurks, pounces, races, and plays dead whenever he thinks it's to his advantage. Yet every time, the fox slinks away defeated, its tender nose pricked by spines. The fox never learns that the hedgehog knows how to do one big thing great -- defend itself.

The *Hedgehog Concept* helps guide you through the process of identifying precisely what you can be great at. This exercise can be done alone or, better yet, as a team involving peers, employees, trusted individuals, etc. Ultimately, you want to land on exactly what it is you do best and how you can differentiate yourself from competition.

The *Hedgehog Concept* sounds simple enough but for it to work you really need to be honest, open, and willing to accept that your current thinking may be well-intended but it's actually way wide of the mark. If you choose to go through this type of soul-searching activity, it's best to start by taking your ego and tossing it into a nearby river!

During my time at Johnson & Johnson, the one question that dominated every division was, "How do you sell new products while at the same time protecting your core business?" Perfectly valid question, right?

Maybe not.

I believe a better question would have been, "How do we leverage what we are *already* good or great at [our core business] to introduce new products that help our customers be more successful?"

It's a simple, subtle twist in wordplay but a very significant one. [It might help to re-read the previous two paragraphs.]

Too many times, J&J would launch new products that truth be told were really just line extensions or gaps in our existing portfolio. Sometimes, it was the wrong product launched on false market assumptions [hence the need for a clear Value Proposition]. Other times it was going into new markets with the same salesforce. [Word of warning: If you have a salesforce that's good at what they do, or hopefully great, they will resist a new type of buyer. Especially if it is more difficult and requires more effort. I saw this over and over again.]

Let's take a look at a company with a great Value Proposition: Uber. At its fundamental level, Uber gets you from Point A to Point B via a few taps on a smart screen or keyboard and a nearby driver. There's no need to exchange money the traditional way and with pre-pickup fare estimates, there are no worries about a taxi driver taking you on a scam route to drive up the fare. Further, Uber offers great flexibility for both parties involved – the passenger[s] and the driver.

It's a New World way of hailing a cab. And it works! Uber is unique, wildly popular, and has definitely entered into the mainstream of many Americans' lives. Uber did an excellent job of laying out their Value Proposition in the early days of its existence.

Uber knew there existed a need [a better way to get to Point B]. It came up with a unique way to fill that need [online]. And it does so at a fair price [though some might think otherwise, at times].

For your salespeople to be successful, you must have a well-crafted, thoughtful Value Prop and they must be able to articulate your company's and/or product's Value Proposition in a sentence or two. The best and most consistently successful salespeople do this.

So, here's an exercise to help you home in on precisely what your Value Proposition is. Ask yourself:

1. *Who are all the stakeholders for your product? [For example, if you sell shoes, it's the owner of the footwear business, the store manager, the salesperson, and the customer.]*

2. *How will your product benefit each stakeholder?*

3. *How will your product help your customer be more successful and make them more money?*

4. *How does your product differ in a way that sets you apart from your competition?*

5. *Will your product save time, money, effort, etc.? How does it do that?*

Once you've answered these questions honestly and satisfactorily, and rolled it out to your sales force, it would be a great idea for you to ride along with a few of your salespeople. See if they are consistently and clearly articulating your company's and/or product's Value Proposition. Odds are it's *not* consistent or clear. Fix this ASAP!

Again, it is critically important your salespeople articulate their Value Proposition sharply and confidently to your customers. If a salesperson doesn't come across as being 100% clear about the Value Prop, it's 100% likely your customer will be confused as well. Not a great way to till the soil for success. The role of the Sales Manager is to make sure your customer-facing representatives are delivering the Value Prop well … and closing deals.

One final point: If you struggle finding good answers to the five questions above, you may be in trouble. It may be time to reassess whether or not this business is viable and is actually going to make it. Best to cut your losses early if you come to the point of having to admit, well, your baby is a tad ugly. You won't be alone.

A whopping 42% of small businesses in the U.S. fail because there's *no market need* for their products. [Or if there is a need, it wasn't made obvious why a particular product is better than everyone else's.] This is an amazing statistic. Nearly *half* of all businesses launched had zero shot to succeed … even before starting!

Don't be one of them. Get your Value Proposition right.

"If your customer base is aging with you, then eventually you are going to become obsolete and irrelevant. You need to be constantly figuring out who are your new customers and what you are doing to stay young forever." – Jeff Bezos

CHAPTER 2

ACQUIRING NEW CUSTOMERS

In my dealings with many small-business owners, I find they struggle with the customer acquisition part of business ... if they do it at all.

Customer acquisition ... rather important, wouldn't you think?

Without *new* customers, your business is doomed to fail. As Jeff Bezos points out above, an "aging in place" strategy for any organization is a fast-track to failure. It's just a matter of time.

An existing business typically has a set number of customers that "pay the bills" or "keep the lights on". To take your business to the next level – to thrive, not merely survive -- it's incumbent on you to attract, acquire and keep *new* customers. And do it over and over and over again.

But how?

Certainly the ways to attract new customers are limitless and with a little imagination you could probably knock out your own list of approaches that work. But in the interest of time and freebie insight, allow me to share a few tips on how to get started.

Determine who your potential customers are then rank them in order of importance. -- Yes, yes, yes, all customers – big or small – are important and it's even *more* important that you treat all customers with the same degree of respect and appreciation. When I say "order of importance", I'm talking about ranking the upside potential of each customer, as measured by potential revenue.

Specifically, I'm talking about assessing the opportunity – potential sales revenue and likelihood of conversion. I'm drawn to visuals like most people so I would plot prospects by assign each to an appropriate box in the quad-split chart below:

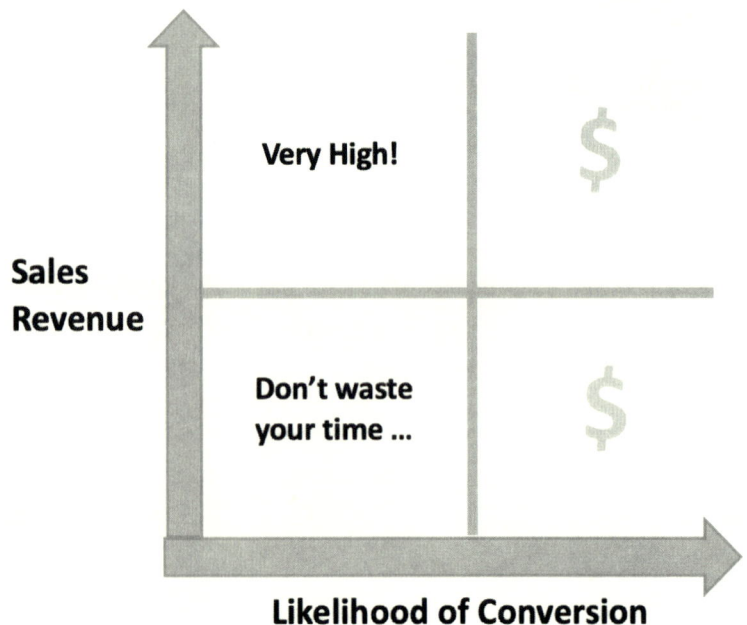

As you can see, you should be targeting customers on the right side of the vertical axis in the chart [where the $ signs are]. Consider the bottom-right quadrant to be low-hanging fruit and the top-right quadrant to be where your whales [your big opportunities] hang out.

Everything left of the vertical axis, hey, knock yourself out if you've got a ton of extra time on your hands or believe your dollar will win the PowerBall.

We'll address the importance of ranking the importance of each potential customer in greater detail in Chapter 5 [*Targeting – Fill the Holes*].

Never underestimate the value of cold-calling -- I've spent most of my career in the medical-device sector. Whenever we recruited new sales representatives, we put a high value on candidates with strong business-to-business [B2B] backgrounds.

Why ...? Because a typical B2B salesperson starts out by cold-calling customers. That's tough stuff, not something just anyone is willing to do.

Let's take, for example, a new copier salesperson. They're assigned a geographical area in which to sell their copiers. They find a large office building in their territory and start at the top floor [where the bigger dollar companies typically reside], knocking on doors to see if anyone is in the market for a copier. And they work their way down, floor by floor.

The sales rep hopes and prays [especially if they're working on a commission-only or commission/draw basis] a business has just moved in and is in need of a copier. Or that they have an old copier and are interested in upgrading to a newer model.

Admittedly, this isn't exactly a targeted approach, much less a hyper-targeted approach. But it pays dividends. A more targeted approach will come at a later time as the rep gains more experience and sharpens his or her sixth sense for potential customers. It's more like playing a "numbers game". The thinking is: "The more people I see, the more likely I will make a sale." Quantity versus quality of targets for now.

Sales reps that stay in this type of job at least two years develop thick skin, as well as the skill to plow through rejection after rejection along the route to a target who says, "Why, yes. I do need a new copier. Let's chat."

Also, these B2Bers learn how to make a great first impression. They know they have a minimum amount of time to maximize their initial impression and capture the prospect's attention quickly. The first couple of years serve as Boot Camp for sales people.

As a business owner, you, too, need to have elements of this cold-calling approach in the Customer Acquisition section of your business plan. It should be part of your day-to-day activities.

While I truly believe targeting or hyper-targeting the right customer is critical for long-term success, the "shotgun approach" is also needed. Reality is, sometimes the greatest sales results tumble from a by chance/happenstance encounter. These are like lucky lotto days where it all boils down to being in the right place at the right time with a dash of serendipity tossed in for good measure.

Maybe that dollar you wasted on a PowerBall ticket wasn't wasted at all!

Execute relentlessly -- Once you identify your target customers, it is through relentless execution [discussed in greater detail in Chapter 6 – *Execution*] that targets become new customers and new customers become repeat customers and repeat customers become long-term customers.

In a blue sky world, you never stop enhancing the two-way respect and bond between your customer and you. And you do this by never failing to execute relentlessly. Having the ol' "under-promise and over-deliver" mentality never hurts, either.

Seek referrals ... many, many referrals -- I believe a part of your day should be dedicated to calling new customers, but the majority of your sales day should be calling on customers to whom you've been referred. Especially since a referral is 10X more likely to close a deal than a shot-in-the-dark customer.

You can garner referrals through existing customers, friends, neighbors, colleagues and former colleagues, fellow business owners, at social gatherings and networking events, etc. [Side note: When you do receive a referral or an introduction to a prospect, be sure to follow up with the person who did you the favor and let them know how things are going.]

Another thing to keep in mind is that referrals can come from those establishments or organizations you patronize in your daily life. For instance, I am a customer at many different restaurants, a gym, a primary-care physician, a dentist, a landscaping company, an exterminating company, a barbershop, a dry cleaner, a grocery store, a pharmacy, you get the picture. Think of how many face-to-face interactions and opportunities you have to ask for referrals as you simply go about your day-to-day life.

You may be surprised how willing these people are to help you. I've long held the belief that people are born with an innate desire to help others. [Even Ebeneezer Scrooge came around in the end!] And if they're not in a position to directly help you, they are typically eager to find someone who can. This is especially true in the case of those businesses you've personally supported, thereby helping the owners put food on the table for their families.

Finally, your LinkedIn connections can be a great source of referrals. When you use LinkedIn in your business-building efforts, be sure to go beyond just tapping into your first level of connections and seek opportunities with second-level connections, as well.

Leverage social media – In addition to LinkedIn, social media and its countless platforms can be very helpful in acquiring new customers, as well as building your referral base. My favorite way is to use "influencers" in your circle and have them endorse/like/comment on your company or brand. Endorsements from key trusted mutual friends or industry leaders is powerful.

We used to use the term "word-of-mouth" referrals and they certainly do still occur but more and more in this rapidly changing world we live in, it's "word-of-technology/social-media" referrals.

Young, tech-bred, tech-savvy people today are "killin' it" in business, using social media to sell products and services without even leaving their homes. You need to attack this area! Dedicate a fair amount of your time leveraging social-media networks. It will definitely help you identify targets, gain endorsements, and land new customers.

Form strategic alliances -- My final tip to you is to form strategic alliances with other companies that sell to your targets or existing customers.

For example, if you sell coffee to small businesses, you may want to find other B2B sales people that sell items or services to your targets or customers [i.e., copiers, HR software, janitorial services, office supplies, insurance, furniture, etc.].

Provide these strategic allies an incentive to give you leads and be prepared to return the favor. In the world of sales, mutual back-scratching is a beautiful, beautiful thing! Forming the right strategic partnerships can help take your business to the next level.

Key Takeaways

1. Make new-customer acquisition a priority.

2. Hire door-knockers/B2Bers.

3. Leverage all your contacts to increase referral business.

4. Leverage social media and influencers.

5. Form strategic partnerships.

"By failing to prepare, you are preparing to fail." – Benjamin Franklin

CHAPTER 3

Q: WHY DO SALES PEOPLE FAIL?

A: Three simple reasons:

1. Lack of preparation

2. Lack of preparation and ...

3. [You guessed it] Lack of preparation

So, why *don't* salespeople prepare enough? The short and simple answer is: It's extra work! And that's the truth. After all, sales folks are busy folks and who needs more line items on the To Do list? Also in many cases, they simply [and sadly] have not been coached on how to best prepare for a sales call.

So, what is it that separates the average performer from a great performer? Bottom line: Preparation, preparation and more PREPARATION. [Did I say that loud enough?] It really is that simple.

Think of elite athletes. The Michael Jordans and Tom Bradys and Serena Williams of the world. Preparation is an ongoing priority, sometimes at the expense of other parts of the athlete's life. It never stops -- pre-season, mid-season, post-season and off-season ... if there ever really is an off-season for these mega-driven individuals. Their preparation is complete and comprehensive. It involves physical training, mental homework, nutrition, sleep as a priority, meditation, film study, visioning, etc.

The biggest of games or events are won by those who put in the time and effort to train, those willing to give it the "blood, sweat and tears" as they say. Same applies to your sales organization.

Next time you're riding along with one of your salespeople to visit a customer, ask: "How did you prepare for this particular sales call?" If you get a blank stare, chances of a successful outcome are not good. To a man or woman, the top performers I worked with were *always* the best prepared.

To this day, I remember the best-prepared sales call I ever experienced. It occurred back in [year or estimated year]. The objective of the sales rep's call was to highlight, demonstrate and sell our new product. She knew our competitor had a 90% market share and understood they were entrenched.

The rep greeted the customer [an Emergency Room Supervisor at a very busy hospital], introducing herself and me. She knew exactly what product this customer used and who the key influencers were in the account. She also had a good idea of their volume, as well as our competitor's strengths and weaknesses compared to ours.

After a few qualifying questions [which she already knew the answers to], we got to the product demo. She did a great job on the demonstration, pointing out *our* strengths and highlighting things their current product [our competitor's] lacked. The customer was obviously very impressed and interested but said, to move forward, we'd need to earn the approval of key doctors in the department.

"Super Rep" already knew who these doctors were and had pre-sold them prior to this appointment and received their endorsement. She validated this by asking the customer if Doctors A, B and C were the ones who needed to approve our product. The customer confirmed and was again very impressed with the rep's intense preparation.

Bullseye! You could actually see the look of excitement on the customer's face. We'd just made her job a lot easier with this product conversion.

So, what do you think happened next?

Well, the customer said she was willing to move forward and asked us to send her a proposal. "Super Rep" responded by asking the customer if they still belonged to XYZ purchasing group. [Again, she already knew they did.] The customer confirmed this and "Super Rep" handed over pre-prepared pricing for the product and a cross-referenced guide with a recommended purchase amount. She also confirmed our price would be lower than competition.

Without skipping a beat, the customer requested a free sample to trial, and "Super Rep" willingly agreed. She told the customer we had a no-loss guarantee and was happy to provide them with enough product for one month at no cost. All she needed was a Purchase Order and, if for some reason the trial was not successful, they could return any unused product.

So they not only got a no-loss guarantee and a better price, they'd be saving money during the freebie trial period. And as you know, hospitals these days are all about saving money. The customer even confirmed we were priced lower than competition and was very eager to test-drive something better, supported by key stakeholders, and save money in the process.

Brilliant, a closed deal. *Next!*

What I love most about this sales call was how thoroughly the sales representative did her homework. Meeting with key doctors before the call likely reduced the sales cycle by a full 60 days. Also, having pricing information ready to hand over on the spot was critical. This cut the sales cycle by at least two more weeks. If she hadn't had this information at the ready, she would have needed to set up another appointment or email the information at a later time.

As busy as people are these days, pricing via email would not be a priority for them and who knows how long it might have been before she took the time to open the document and analyze the pricing ... if ever?

In total, I would estimate "Super Rep" accelerated the sales cycle by 60-90 days with her level of preparation. In a word, that is *awesome*. A better product at a lower price. Our company gained incremental profit, not to mention stature in the product category. And the rep was rewarded with a new account and the compensation that goes with it. Clearly, a win for all.

Imagine closing *all* your sales deals three months faster than the typical elongated cycle. How successful would your company be and how successful would *you* be?

I'm here to tell you, it's possible. You can do this. When you prioritize and focus on relentless, intense preparation -- tailored specifically to the individual needs of each customer -- I promise you will increase the frequency of closed deals and significantly reduce the number of days needed to do it. Below is a checklist of the type of information you'll need to make that happen:

- What are your **current sales** in this account?

- What is the **total sales potential** for the account?

- Who are the **key decision-makers**? [Typically, there's more than one. The savvy salesperson understands this and knows who all the key influencers, as well as their "hot buttons". If you *don't* know this, find out or ask someone who does.]

- Who are **your competitors**? This is key as you will need to expertly position your product versus competition. An "apples-to-apples" comparison opens the door to an "apples-to-BETTER-apples" outcome. This is one of the most important things you can do because most people innately resist change. That's why it's incumbent upon *you* to give them a solid reason to embrace a change.

- Who are **your customers' customers**? This is important because it demonstrates to your customer that you understand their business at an insightful, meaningful level. Also, you may be able to help them with intel and trends for their business.

- Who are **your customers' competitors**? One of the strongest values you can bring to your customer is intel on their competition. At Johnson & Johnson, our customers valued and wanted this information. They knew we called on many like-customers and were interested in learning of competitors' "benchmark practices" for their toughest challenges, as well as any trends we were monitoring in the marketplace.

- **Utilize Google alerts** on your customers and your customers' customers. This keeps you informed of their most recent activities and happenings. It demonstrates to your customers that you have an active, ongoing interest in their business. This goes a long way in fostering the trust you need to close a deal.

- **Scour your customers' websites** as well as the websites of competitors.

- **Regularly update each of your customers' profiles** – i.e., personality style, time in each position, where they're from, schools they attended, hobbies, special interests, number of children, favorite sports team, hot buttons, priorities, etc. The more you know about them, the more likely you'll be quick on your feet in conversation and welcomed into their circle.

- **Read industry publications**, especially those you know your customer reads.

Bottom Line: **Preparation + Preparation = Success + Success** It really is that simple.

"Be quick to listen, slow to speak." – James 1:19

CHAPTER 4

YOUR SELLING PROCESS

Truly effective selling is a well-thought-out series of steps required to demonstrate your product to the target or customer so you can close the deal. It is no different than any other thing requiring a procedure or process manual. Think of it as your road map to success or, if you're targeting "whales", your treasure map to success.

It's up to you to follow the road map to reach your destination or use the clues to discover the treasure chest. [And don't forget to have some fun along the way.]

One of my favorite movies is *My Cousin Vinny*. A greenhorn personal injury attorney, Vinny Gambini travels from Brooklyn to rural Alabama to represent his cousin who has been wrongfully accused of the murder of a convenience store clerk. It's "Brooklyn brash" versus "Southern gentility". Vinny is consistently held in contempt of court early in the movie for not following court procedure.

His fiancée, Mona Lisa Vito, becomes very concerned and is baffled as to why Vinny didn't learn this in law school. Fully aware of his inexperience and shortcomings in court procedure and protocol, Vinny tries to explain to Mona Lisa that procedure is taught by the hiring law firm [he has yet to be hired by a firm since graduating], not law school. He goes on to explain court procedure is similar to rebuilding a carburetor.

"The first thing you do is you take the carburetor off the manifold. Suppose you skip the first step, and while you're replacing one of the jets, you accidentally drop the jet. It goes down the carburetor, rolls along the manifold, and goes into the head. You are [expletive]!"

She somewhat agrees and is hopeful she won't need to bail him out much more. Turns out Vinny *does* have an understanding of the importance of process.

Having been on thousands of sales calls, I am always amazed at how the majority of salespeople don't follow the formal and logical steps of the selling process/procedure. Most want to immediately jump into the product demonstration. While each company tailors the sales process to best fit their particular product and its sales cycle, there are universal steps regardless.

There have been literally thousands of books written on sales. [Yes, this among them.] Go to any local book store or shop online and you'll see multitudes of sales guides and manuals with catchy titles. Below are some of my favorites. And by the way, they're all classics that have stood the test of time and there's a reason why:

- *The Greatest Salesman in the World* [Og Mandino] -- This is the first book I read and re-read as a young salesperson. While it does not lay out a true sales process, it delivers a great message and is highly motivating.

- *Secrets of Closing the Sale* [Zig Ziglar] -- This is another early book I read. Many tips on examples of closing a sale, as well as great stories from Zig.

- *The Psychology of Selling* [Brian Tracey] -- Brian has written many books and released many audio segments. I used to listen to his segments as well as refer to this book often for insight and refreshers on sales tips.

- *Integrity Selling* [Ron Willingham] -- This is my favorite and the one most utilized by divisions of Johnson & Johnson for initial sales training. Its sales process is easy to follow and flows very naturally.

After having read and re-read these books many times, and after being witness to thousands of sales calls, I can very easily summarize the universal message in all: **KEEP THE PROCESS SIMPLE.** And as we covered in detail in Chapter 3, your salespeople *must* begin with diligent preparation. Here we go ...

A SIMPLE SALES PROCESS

1. **INTRODUCTION** – Get the room temperature and state exactly why you are here.

2. **ASK PROBING QUESTIONS** to identify the customer's needs.

3. **DEMONSTRATE** how your product meets their needs [as revealed in Step 2].

4. **STOP-PAUSE.** Ask, "What do you think so far?" [Word of Caution: Based on the customer's response, you may need to think fast and course-correct or execute a full U-turn in your messaging.]

5. **HANDLE OBJECTIONS AND ADDRESS CONCERNS.** Face them straight on with facts and relevant data.

6. **CLOSE.** Ask for a sale. Amazingly, this is the step most often neglected. It's important for you to leave each call with a firm decision ... hopefully a "yes" but often a "no". Know where you stand after every call and go back to do more homework if you haven't – *yet* -- closed the deal.

Let's dive a bit deeper into each of these steps.

1. **INTRODUCTION: State Your Purpose**
"Why are you here?" is what your prospect is thinking when you enter their office. They may also be thinking:

> *"Hey, I'm busy, my boss is demanding, I have issues on the home front, I could lose my job, my mother just received a bad diagnosis, I just left a*

meeting and our expenses are out of control, I can't wait to go on vaca-
tion next week, I hate this job, I need to call my recruiter, I hate sales-
people, I love salespeople that give me free stuff ..."

... or any of the other 12,000-50,000 thoughts human beings have each day. Oh, and by the way, 80% of those thoughts are negative. Ensure your own thoughts are upbeat and positive regardless of extenuating circumstances, yours or the customer's.

With this in mind, always assume there may be something on their mind that isn't work-related or have anything to do with you, your product or your company.

Upon arrival, quickly assess the "temperature" in the room. You do this mostly through observation. A good tip is to ask the administrative assistant before stepping into the meeting, "How are things? Busy, slow ...?"

I always try to make an immediate connection with the potential buyer by either commenting or asking about something in their office – a diploma, an award, an interesting object, a family photo from a recent vacation, a Bible on the shelf, an inspirational quote on the desk, etc. Always seek to find a common ground, such as attending the same school, hailing from the same state or city, a shared ethnicity or nationality at birth, etc. [If you did your pre-planning correctly, you will already have some of this info.]

Almost instantaneously, the customer will form an opinion of you as you enter the room. Make sure it's positive. Be neatly groomed. Smile. Make eye contact. Stand upright, extend a warm handshake, and speak with a sincere tone that shows respect, confidence and humility.

Some say you have as long as seven seconds to make that first impression but research shows it's actually less than that. Like it or not, immediately sizing someone up is simple human nature. And as Will Rogers once said, "You never get a second chance to make a first impression." Truth.

If someone has made a referral on your behalf, you're a step closer to being able to close a deal. A referral is the absolute best way to make a connection as noted in Chapter 2. Gaining referrals is strangely underutilized in sales and something I feel may be the most important tactic in developing trust with the customer. Someone has endorsed you so you're automatically afforded an extra degree of validation and respect.

In a normal [if there is such a thing] sales call, the very fact a call was scheduled is proof the customer hopes that what you have to sell or demonstrate will be of interest and value to them. After all, they've gifted you 30-60 minutes of their precious time. Congratulations!

Assuming you're meeting with a qualified buyer who has decision-making power to purchase your product [or influence the acceptance of your product], you've accomplished what I feel is the most difficult step – earning the audience. The stage is set for you to show how your product meets their needs. If you do that effectively, you will succeed in closing a deal.

Let's talk about trust.

Gaining a customer's trust is one of the biggest hurdles you'll need to clear once in the door, if not the biggest. Your No.1 job is to earn the trust of your customer. Those that are able to do this are consistent winners. Also, expressing gratitude for the customer's time is critically important. It goes a long way towards proving to the customer you respect them.

Your opening statement should be as simple as, "Thank you for taking the time to meet with me/us today," then **STATE YOUR PURPOSE**! Answer the unspoken question, "Why are you here?" Make it short, to the point and state some benefit to the customer.

My Professor of Sales at the University of Miami used to describe benefit in the sales process as "ME-nefit". As in "What's in it for me?" It's a fair question for the customer to ask so be sure you're prepared to answer.

Before you begin the blah-blah-blah "verbal diarrhea" about your product and its benefits/ME-nifits, open with pertinent questions. My thought process when meeting with a customer or prospect is always, "How can I help *them* be more successful? Will my product help them make more money, or save them money? Will it save them time? Improve their brand? Help their customers?"

Putting yourself on the other side of the desk will help guide your approach. After all, their success is your success.

I often use an analogy from the basketball movie *Hoosiers*. In the movie, Coach Dale requires his players to pass the ball a minimum four times before shooting. The reason for this is, first and foremost, you're likely to create a better opening for a shot and, second, you tire the defense a bit more by making them work a little harder.

When I was in sales leadership roles, I asked my salespeople to ask four questions before ever pulling the product or promotional materials out of the bag. Of course, there are exceptions to this – like when the customer is in a hurry and you only have five minutes, or when something arises during the meeting that abruptly ends your visit. That's when you need to quickly and clearly articulate your Value Proposition ... then get out of their way for today.

Let's say I'm selling wine to a restaurant. Success to a restaurant operator is defined as more customers coming into their restaurant more often and spending more money. Further, it's developing and maintaining a great reputation for quality at a fair price. Operators also want to retain their top employees who are critical in attracting and retaining customers. Servers connect with diners and vice-versa.

Your Purpose Statement could be:

"Hi, [Customer Name]. My name is Joe and I represent Moonshine Wine. We're working with top restaurants in the area utilizing customizable concepts to help drive customers to your restaurant and increase revenues based on your clientele."

Note the key words and phrases here:

- **Working with top restaurants ...**
  [Translation: You operate a first-class restaurant.]

- **Customizable ...**
  [Translation: Tailored to your needs.]

- *Drive customers and revenue ...*
[Translation: Help you make more money.]

So if I told you, "Hey, you're at the top of your industry, you're in demand, and I want to help you make more money," would you be curious and interested to learn more? Of course, you would! Without bloviating, appeal to the customer's ego and be sure your delivery is smooth and sincere ... not like that of a gushing, pushy used car salesperson.

After stating your purpose, begin by asking well-thought-out questions. Here are a few examples:

- *"How are things at [company name]? How has business been?"*

- *"How long have you worked at [company name]?"*

- *Are there any major/key projects you're currently working on or coming up soon?"* FYI: The answer to this question may help you better navigate the conversation and/or position your product for a sale. Again, if you are prepared, you may already have the answer.

- *"So, where are you from originally?"* If they're friendly or open, I eventually get to this question at some point in the presentation. Sharing a common birthplace or hometown or rooting interest in a sports teams goes a long way towards establishing a connection.

Be sure to:

1. Pre-plan.

2. Set the appointment.

3. Dress for success – Keep in mind industry and company culture.

4. Arrive 15 minutes early and use that time to review your questions and your call objective.

5. Greet gatekeepers and take the "temperature" of the room.

2. **– ASK PROBING QUESTIONS: Uncover their needs via SWOT**
   [Strengths, Weaknesses, Opportunities and Threats]

   - **Question 1:** "How is business?"
     - o **Question 2A** [If they say "good" or "great"]: "What's your secret?"

     - o **Question 2B**: [If they say "bad"]: "What do you attribute that to?"

   - **Question 3**: "Are there any cool things you're doing right now to attract more customers or increase ticket totals?"

   - **Question 4**: "What has worked or not worked for you in the past?"

   - **Question 5**: "What do you see as your biggest barrier to growth?"

By now, you should have a sense of their current state of affairs. You must delicately probe a bit more to find out why and what they're doing to keep it going or to improve it? Find out if they have new menu items planned or if they're going to run specials.

Once you've completed a SWOT approach with your customer, you can better position your product and messaging to meet their most pressing needs. Only by truly understanding your customers' main challenges in driving revenue and reducing costs will you be able to close the sale.

In any Profit & Loss [P&L] statement, you will see the top line is "Revenue". This is No.1 for a reason. How do you help them increase their revenue?

The second most important line on the P&L is "Expenses". How will your product help them reduce expenses? Most salespeople focus too much on the second line. Sales reps that do not probe enough to uncover the real needs of their customers typically crumble under price objection.

When the customer says, "Your price is too high" or "We can't afford this," the rep will immediately default to the lowest price to try to get the sale. This may be successful in the short term but over time you erode your margins and only keep the business until someone else comes in at a lower price. Essentially, you've wasted all your pricing leverage too early in the game. In the absence of perceived value, price becomes the only factor in the customer's decision to buy or decline.

I firmly believe one of the best tactics you can deploy to really uncover your customer's needs is to get them outside of their place of business. I always felt lunch or dinner meetings provided a friendlier, more open atmosphere for a discussion. Also, if they attend a trade show, meet them there and invite them to dinner, lunch or breakfast. Do something fun. A sporting event is always good if they're so inclined.

3. **DEMONSTRATE: Make your presentation**
Hey, it's *your* story, tell it well.

Now that the salesperson has uncovered the customer's needs, it's time to tell your story. What I mean by that is you'll need to demonstrate to them how and why your product will meet and exceed their needs.

This is where it's critically important for your sales reps know their product "up-down and inside-out", as they say. They should be able to quickly articulate how your product addresses the "ME-nefits" – essentially, answering "What's in it for me?]. The more technical your product or service, the more important this is. Having managed sales reps in highly technical and non-technical products, I cannot emphasize this enough.

Buyers, especially those who are competent and experienced, can immediately tell when you don't know your stuff. I have seen sales reps lose credibility in seconds by not knowing their product inside and out. And by the way, it's not only important to know *your* product, but your competitor's as well. It is also critical you spend a great deal of time in product training [yours and your competitor's]. A division I once worked for required 90 days of product training before you ever spoke to your first customer. This may seem like a long time but, I assure you, we were definitely ready after three months of intense training.

One of the best salespeople I had the pleasure to coach was also my most technically sound team member. He was the best in the country. He knew his product and our competitor's product expertly.

He'd typically begin by asking the customer what they were currently using/buying. The computer in his brain worked in milliseconds. He knew his competitors so well that he immediately knew their weaknesses, who represented their line [important to know if the competitive rep is good or weak]. If the competitive rep was weak, this definitely opened a door. If the competitive rep was good, he instantly acknowledged it and this would build his own credibility. *Never slam the competition.* Be diplomatic when you point out weaknesses by using "watch outs" when speaking of the competition.

At this stage, less is more, but you need to make sure you position your product based specifically on the customer's needs. Also, don't waste time explaining features or benefits they're not interested in.

A piece of leave-behind literature can help reinforce what you've just explained to them, or for them to refresh their memory. Having said that, I often discourage leaving a sales aid behind unless the customer requests one since they usually go in the garbage if not requested. Also, in this day of technology and the emphasis on "going green", it's probably better to follow-up later in the day or the next day [at the very latest] with a follow-up email and attached sales aid. It shows good follow-through and affords you another point-of-contact immediately after the initial sales call.

When demonstrating your product, it is very important to do so in the context of the customer's needs. Let's say you're a shoe sales representative and you learned the prospect you're selling shoes to has too much unsold inventory on hand and they're thinking of cutting back on purchasing new inventory. They also mention they're having difficulty retaining sales clerks, much less motivating the ones they have.

Based on too much inventory and too little retention, here would be my demonstration:

"The shoe I'd like to show you today is doing really well in many of my stores. And, we're doing a major promotion soon! I'm confident your customers will be seeking our new shoe.

"I am happy to be here the day the shipment arrives and work the floor with your team to show them the most effective way to sell this particular shoe. I can also provide an incentive to your top producer."

If you notice, I did not start with features and benefits of the actual shoe. I began with addressing the concerns I'd uncovered by probing before presenting. This tills the soil for more open-mindedness and receptivity on the part of the customer.

4. **STOP- PAUSE: "What do you think so far?"**

It is time to stop your demonstration and ask the most important question before getting to "the ask": "So Jim, tell me what you think so far ..."

This allows the customer to digest what has been presented, to stop and think, then give you his or her true feelings/objections/concerns. Let's continue to play out the scenario ...

Jim: "Joe, I like the shoe, but I need to run down my inventory before I order it. I love the idea of you being here to help my guys sell and provide them an incentive though."

Joe: "What type of incentive or incentives do you think your guys would like?"

Jim: "They love gift cards."

Joe – "Perfect. We can make that happen!"

Start thinking of the solution for the inventory problem. Jim likes the shoe and likes your idea of training his team and providing an incentive. You now need to ...

5. HANDLE OBJECTIONS AND CONCERNS

In this case, it's too much inventory and inadequate training, leading to low employee retention. It's now what I call FEEL-FELT-FOUND time. This is one of the best, if not the best way, to overcome an objection. Here's how it works:

FEEL – "Jim, I understand how you feel about inventory." [You acknowledge what his concerns and do not just blow it off.]

FELT – "Many of my customers have felt the same way." [This shows he's not alone. Buyers like to feel they're getting as good a deal as the other guy, or that others are experiencing similar struggles.]

FOUND – What they found was that having the right inventory on-hand was critical for their success as well as increasing revenue. Thus, you explain, "Jim, this is the right shoe, with the right promotional incentives with training for your folks. Let's give it a shot."

Jim: "I don't know, Joe. I'm still not sure ..."

At this point, if they continue to harp on their current inventory challenges, offer a way to help them. Do your research. [Remember that *Preparation-Preparation-PREPARATION* thing?]

According to market-research experts, sitting inventory can lose up to 2% of its value *per week*. If this is the case, encourage him to do a fire sale with slow movers. Incentivize his folks to move these out of the store, thus making room for the new and better inventory.

In overcoming objections, it's the solution that matters most. That's why you need to know not only your product, but have a keen grasp of business solutions – what works and what doesn't.

The FEEL-FELT-FOUND approach is one of the best ways to overcome objections and ease concerns. It is in overcoming objections where sales are won and lost. The high-performing salesperson is very comfortable in this stage of the selling process for two reasons:

---

1. They know their product inside and out and have already anticipated objections and concerns.

2. They truly believe their product is the very *best* solution for their customers. Belief in your product is critical to any salesperson's success.

After you've progressed through the PAUSE stage then moved through the HANDLE OBJECTIONS AND CONCERNS stage, you are poised to advance matters to the final stage in which you gain commitment and CLOSE the sale. The "What do you think so far?" has enabled you to uncover objections early, as well as provide the opportunity to tailor or reposition your story based on the customer's stated objections and concerns [similar to a movie director yelling, "Cut!" in the middle of a scene].

Before we move on, I truly believe when you're able to accurately assess the "room temperature", ask the proper probing questions, and tell your story well, closing the sale is just a formality. Think of it as going into the victory formation and running out the clock at the end of a football game.

And for the record, I love stories and football games with happy endings!

6. **– CLOSE: As for the order.**

Asking for the order is very simple … so why it so daunting to so many?

Does it feel as if you'll be encroaching on someone's space, being too pushy or forward? Does it come off as demanding or presumptious? Will kittens and puppies perish if the customer stalls you or delivers a flat-out "No, not right now"?

No, no and no. No on all counts! Quite the opposite, actually.

Asking for the business implies you're confident, you truly believe earned the right to ask the question, and you genuinely want to help that person and their business be more successful and, thus, more profitable. That's what the CLOSE or the ASK is at its core.

Though I'm not really a fan of this approach, some people find great success leapfrogging over the first question and moving to the second: "So, [Name], how many would you like?" In my mind, it can come across as a bit arrogant and, indeed, presumptuous. Certain personality types can pull it off, though.

I much prefer what I call the "summary" CLOSE. In this case, you summarize all the points that were agreed upon and vslidate for the customer they're about to make a solid business decision. If we go back to the shoe example, it would go like this:

> "Jim, I'm glad I'll be able to be here to help your team drive sales of our new shoe. We discussed your current excess inventory and how a special promo for the slow movers, along with an incentive for your top-performer, will help you free up some cash. Finally, by having our shoe available shortly, you can take advantage of the early promotional price and our media push this spring.

> "Here's my order form with the most common sizes, based on what you've told me in the past. Does this look about right? Cool. I will put the order in and you should have everything in less than two weeks. This will give you time to push out your excess inventory and be ready prior to our ad campaign. Thank you for your business and I'll see you in a couple of weeks!"

Another one of my favorite closes is, "What's it going to take?"

This is a more aggressive CLOSE and should only be utilized when it's obvious the client wants to buy ... but uses price as the main objection. I once had a customer who really wanted our product but our competitor had a lower price. I asked them, "So, what price is it going to take?"

He threw out a number I knew we would never match but I thought, "What if I could save him the same amount on something else he wasn't already buying from us?" Indeed, we had another product that I knew we could be more price-flexible with, so I gave him that as an option and he agreed. Remember, "No" doesn't always mean "No". But it does require you having a Plan B.

Another close is the "either-or" style. Would you like it in green or blue? Do you want to order it next-day or standard delivery? Be careful though, you don't ever want to come across as pushy or desperate.

Okay, that's a very quick overview of the sales process. To summarize [I told you I like the "summary" CLOSE so that's how I'll conclude this chapter], it all starts with research done *prior* to the call. Once you're on the sales call, you need to *follow the sales process*. Think of a great football coach that has a great Game Plan. It means nothing if the players don't execute it.

So, to recap the selling process:

1. **INTRODUCTION:** State you purpose [why you are here].

2. **ASK PROBING QUESTIONS:** Uncover their needs via SWOT.

3. **DEMONSTRATE:** Make your presentation.

4. **STOP-PAUSE :** What do you think so far?

5. **HANDLE OBJECTIONS AND CONCERNS:** FEEL-FELT-FOUND

6. **CLOSE:** Ask for the order.

"If you are aiming at nothing, you will hit it every time." – Zig Ziglar

CHAPTER 5

TARGETING: FILL THE HOLES!

In the older movie *Stand and Deliver*, math professor Jaime Escalante encourages his high school students to "fill the hole" when trying to solve fundamental algebra problems. He equates negative numbers to a hole dug on a sandy beach and positive numbers to a pile of sand on the beach. Sales targeting involves much the same thought process.

Some years back, I had an excellent sales trainer that applied this fundamental concept to successful selling. "Filling the hole" is the first step in sales targeting, he told us. However, most companies offer very little support in this area. In the context of selling, "filling the hole" is assessing which products you're already selling in your accounts and which ones you are not. For instance, if you're currently selling Products A and B in account XYZ -- but *not* Product C – then Product C becomes is "the hole" in account XYZ.

Obviously, it helps any company and sales person to be able to successfully sell the entire portfolio of products but, more than that, it is significantly easier [and less costly] to sell to an *existing* customer than it is to sell to a new one. In fact, studies have shown it's anywhere from 5-25X more expensive to sell to new customers.

The typical company is pretty good about providing product knowledge and training to their new hires. However, when that sales rep concludes training, they're usually thrown into their territory with little to no further direction. And by the way, filling the holes" upon completion of product training is an expectation of management and will be factored into your performance reviews and compensation.

Lack of sales direction is a huge problem for salesforces throughout the world. The problem is most Sales Managers do not work with a new rep until a few months after completion of training. In my opinion, this is one of the biggest mistakes Sales Managers make.

My belief is Sales Managers must be with new reps on calls the very first week after training to provide the direction they need in order to successfully "fill the holes". Most new reps are understandably clueless as to where to go, whom to meet with, and what to sell first.

I'll never forgot a comment a Sales Manager once made to me about working with a rep right after training. He told me the reason he didn't work with new-hire right out of the chute was that he did not want to be with a rep who might get lost while driving to accounts. *Unbelievable!*

His attitude was to let the sales reps "goober around" for a couple of months then once they knew their way around geographically, he would *grace them* with his presence. [Hmmm ... is arrogance spelled with a capital "A" or small "a"?] Basically, this guy didn't want to be inconvenienced and he put his own selfish interests ahead of what was best for the new sales rep. Unfortunately, there are many Sales Managers with this attitude.

Certainly with GPS, Google Maps, Waze and other way-finder software and apps readily available at no cost on phones, in watches and in dashboards, it's basically a non-issue today. While "getting there" has become easier, there's still a problem with executing a successful sales call. It remains critically important, in my never-to-be-humble opinion, that Sales Managers should never throw a new-hire to the wolves and see how he or she does. They should immediately set the rep up for success in the days following competition of training.

In many cases, the rep previously assigned to the designated territory is unavailable to mentor and coach the new-hire for obvious reasons. He or she may have left the company or been terminated, retired, etc. Unless they happen to be of unusually kind heart, they're likely not going to waste time on something that doesn't put money in their wallet.

However, in the case of the previous rep being promoted, moving to a new role within the organization, or being switched to a new territory, they absolutely *should* make themselves available.

In my mind, the role of the Sales Manager is to be a servant to his people and there is no better time to do that than right at the beginning. Earlier in this book, we talked about the "whales". Well, you might be interested to know whale calves are alongside their mothers for the first 6-7 months of life before going off on their own. Of course, no Sales Manager is going to invest *that* amount of time with a new-hire but you get the point: New-hires need to be nurtured and encouraged and shown the right way to survive and thrive in the world. This sets you them up for success with those lucrative "whale" targets down the road.

Back to "filling the hole" ...

Step 1:

Rank accounts in terms of sales potential as well as existing sales. The reason you do this is because many sales reps only rank accounts based on existing sales. Both are important factors in the ranking process. For example:

- Account A currently buys $90,000 in product. Total potential is $100,000.

- Account B purchases $15,000 in product. Total potential is $50,000.

Obviously, Account B has $35,000 of potential new business while Account A has only $10,000. Thus, Account B has more potential than A and if they are an attainable target, time is better spent trying to obtain *that* missing piece of business ... filling *that* specific hole, so to speak.

This is not to say that B deserves *more* time and attention. After all, A is worth $90,000 and B is currently only worth $15,000. The purpose of this exercise is to rank based on sales *potential* in order to provide a "hit list" of products or services your existing accounts can potentially purchase.

Target with urgency and be very focused on answering these questions:

1. Do they need your product today or in the near future? [Also, their potential purchase should be significant, not "small potatoes".]

2. Do they have the resources to purchase at this time or will they in the near future?

3. Is your current point-of-contact a decision-maker or at least a key influencer?

If you got a yes to all three, you're in business!

I was fortunate to be part of a large study on salesforce effectiveness at Johnson & Johnson. We quickly learned that targeting was one area that separated successful reps from weak reps. In this study of 300+ sales reps, each were put into two groups:

- High-Performers [HP] or ...

- Low-Performers [LP]

Here were our findings:

1. HPs actually called on *fewer* customers than LPs. They may have called on fewer customers, but they were calling on the *right* customers. This is successful targeting. Quality versus quantity [like fine wine and friendships].

2. HP's customers were more educated on our products and truly believed in our service. LP's customers believed our service to be average. Again, a savvy customer understands value and considers our HPs to be consultants or partners; truly interested and invested in the customer's growth and profitability. From a targeting perspective,

an educated buyer who seeks and understands true value is a great customer to target.

3. Since HPs saw fewer customers, they knew them more intimately and better understood their issues and challenges in growing their business. This showed us that targeting the *right* customers [those with high-volume potential] and building win/win relationships were keys to long-term growth.

Targeting and planning go hand-in-hand. If you have a new sales person, my suggestion is to place as much emphasis on sales planning and targeting as you do product training.

I attended so many product training sessions where we would spend 90% of our time on the features and benefits of our products then, at the end [usually in a very rushed] someone would tell you, "Oh, here are some targets and here's the new commission plan. Have a great trip home and kick some butt!"

Absolutely *not* the way to do it.

"Most leaders would agree they'd be better off having an average strategy with superb execution than a superb strategy with average execution." – Stephen Covey

CHAPTER 6

EXECUTION

There are few 100% certainties in the human experience but I can sure point out one: All great plans are doomed to fail without action! Of *course* this is common sense but you'd be surprised at how often plans fail due to inaction or incorrect action.

My definition of sales execution is:

**Relentless effort toward
the MISSION of closing targeted business.**

Plain and simple. From start to finish. Nothing is over until it's *over*. Why else would astronauts declare "Mission complete" only *after* success has been achieved?

Like a shark in the water smelling blood, you need to attack with relentless ferocity, day in and day out. To me, EXECUTION and HARD WORK are synonymous. When I coach sales representatives, I challenge them to begin each day by identifying four meaningful IMPACTS. By "IMPACT", I mean a sales call, phone call, email or any other point-of-contact with newly targeted customers.

This dogged daily discipline ensures follow-through and creates a pipeline for growth. We all get busy doing "stuff" but business development needs to be the clear No.1 priority for any sales rep or organization. I believe phone calls and email are the most efficient ways to touch our customers. Both methods save time and help with better qualifying potential targets.

From my experience, the best way to maintain consistent execution is via the dreaded TRACKER. A TRACKER is exactly what the word states, it tracks what you do relative to your biz-development efforts. Be sure to track all activity on your targeted accounts and do it on a weekly basis. Make it an automatic action, one that's embedded in your weekly routine.

Let's say you have two salespeople. For this quarter, each has targeted 10 customer conversions. If you don't have a Customer Relationship Manager [CRM] tool, create an Excel file with:

- Account Name

- Product[s] Targeted

- Sales Potential [as measured by units sold and dollar volume] and ...

- A "Notes"column to record details of your most recent activity

Review this weekly, one rep and one target at a time. Laborious, yes. Fact is, salespeople don't like this but I'm here to tell you it's critical to excellent [if not flawless] execution. As I said a moment ago, we all get very busy and forget that closing business and moving on to the next customer is our ultimate goal. At least, that's what your sales leadership believes and, Lord knows, it's important to keep them happy.

Truth be told, this tracking system makes *everyone* accountable, salesperson and Sales Manager. My suggestion is to do it every Monday morning. This allows you to make suggestions to yourself on tactics to close the business for the week ahead.

Many organizations do these reviews on Fridays, but Fridays tend to be difficult. Most of us are one foot into the weekend by Friday afternoon and who needs one more mandatory "To Do" item after a very busy week? Also, weekends tend to fill with personal activities which means Monday morning rolls around and you're already three days behind.

Another strike against Fridays is the reality that travel snags are often prevalent in the rush to get home and, as a result, calls are often canceled or postponed. People also want to leave early for vacations or have family obligations to tend to on Friday evenings.

Whether you're a Sales Manager or a rep, do yourself a favor and fit these reviews in between your first and second cup of coffee early on Monday morning. You'll not only be glad you did, late-Friday afternoon will look even more enticing to you.

Another reason I like the TRACKER is because it's more science than art. Facts are facts and you can't argue with facts. They're black-and-white and there's no room for 50 shades of gray, or any other hue for that matter.

Salespeople also tend to be pretty crafty at coming up with reasons why their customers aren't buying. But if they're repeating the same issues week after week, you quickly see the pattern and you know you have someone in need of a plan, as well as the diligence and follow-through to work that plan.

It might be they're talking to non-decision-makers or the wrong decision-makers. Maybe they aren't handling objections and concerns well enough, or chasing a target that simply doesn't have room in their budget to do business with you right now. The reasons don't matter, targeting and executing are what ultimately matter.

When I was in the capital business, buyers budgeted big-capital items a year in advance. Typically, capital is a long-range budget item except in cases of emergencies. I once had a sales representative who, after we'd done the TRACKER on her activities for a while, would say: "They're sold on our technology and are going to buy, but final approval is sitting on the CFO's desk."

This went on for two months and eight weekly tracker calls. It had become a broken record. The rep really believed she was merely a CFO signature away from completing a Purchase Order. Since it had already been two months, I suggested she set up a meeting with the CFO and get the real skinny since the Purchasing Agent was of little help pushing this peanut down the road.

Granted, this is a delicate situation. You don't want to go over the buyer's head, but you *can* do it tactfully. I suggested to the rep she set up a meeting with the buyer, CFO, and me. This way, we could make it appear it was boss-to-boss – her boss and her point-of-contact's boss -- which would be less threatening and wouldn't jeopardize their relationship.

In that meeting, we discovered the hospital was losing money and trying to delay purchasing any new capital that wasn't absolutely critical. We also found the hospital had other pressing needs where money originally allocated for our product could be reallocated and better utilized. Now we knew the truth. We had a complete, factual picture instead of an assumption.

Bottom line here was that our sales rep had been kept in the dark. If she'd had the benefit of this insight sooner, she could have created a sense of urgency with the end-user of our product to push the need -- not simply to make a sale and fill our coffers but to demonstrate how our product would save them money in the long-term through greater efficiency, less downtime, reliable service, etc. But since she'd assumed it was budgeted and they were ready to pull the trigger, she didn't sense the need to resell the value of our product at *all* levels within the buyer's organization.

These are the things you pick up from doing the weekly TRACKER calls. In the situation I just shared, we probably should have investigated after one month but the salesperson kept assuring me it was only a matter of time and we assumed we were getting the full picture. [You know what they say about the word "assume".] Turns out, until that meeting, we weren't getting the full picture because we didn't have all the facts.

The other benefit of the TRACKER is that you begin to identify trends. Are the objections starting to sound the same? If so, you may have a positioning or product issue. This is where the data on the TRACKER can help you course-correct, if and when needed.

In summary, to better execute your sales plan:

1. Ensure everyone has an updated business plan with identified targets that will help them overachieve and blow past their quota.

2. Purchase a CRM tool or develop an Excel-based weekly TRACKER system.

3. Set up a weekly call, preferably on Monday mornings.

4. Assess your tracking information and identify emerging patterns, trends and/or common objections as to why you are not closing business.

5. Share successes with other team members.

"In the end, it's about the teaching. What I always loved about coaching was the practices. Not the games, not the tournaments, not the alumni stuff. But teaching the players during practice was what coaching was all about to me." – John Wooden

CHAPTER 7

COACHING

Like it or not, everyone needs a coach.

Imagine a football team taking the field without a coach. [I know, I'm back to sports again. But seriously, there are so many real-world challenges that can be illustrated with sports analogies.] Who would assess the talent, select the starters and assign positions on the Depth Chart? Who would design and implement the Game Plan? Who would make the right calls in pressure situations and substitute the right players?

And what about practice? Who would take the lead and teach players form and technique, and share other valuable insights so the team is better able to compete against high-level competition?

Without coaches, players would still know to line up and snap the ball or rush the opposing team's quarterback but they would undoubtedly struggle with being organized, developing a strategy, play-calling and knowing how and when to "course-correct" or make halftime adjustments if the game isn't tracking to plan.

A timeless adage from coaches in all sports is: "You play like you practice." I would venture, in 99% of all situations, that is true. [I'm hedging a smidge to avoid declaring an absolute. There are, of course, rogue exceptions to every rule.]

If your salespeople aren't being coached – or refuse to practice and study, listen and learn proper technique and form, or resist all coaching efforts in favor of freelancing their own Game Plan -- well, how do you think they're going to perform on the sales call? Trust me, these are not the types you want to wager a bet on in Vegas. The likelihood of failure is significant so don't waste your time and money.

My preferred style of coaching is one that I implemented all the way back when I served as a new Sales Manager. As a very successful sales rep, I was surprised at the skill level and preparation of my new team. After working with all 12 of my new salespeople, I realized why I won so many sales awards. Yes, I was good, maybe even better than good, but maybe it was because everyone else was *not* good!

On one of my ride-along calls with a senior rep, we had a horrible first day. I went with the flow on Day 1 and simply observed. It wasn't easy, but I was in assessment mode. On Day 2, I asked the rep what he had planned and it was a lousy plan – face-to-face follow-up calls [that could have been handled by phone] or calling on small customers with a whole lot of "windshield time" in between stops.

I couldn't take it.

"Stop!" I said. "Let's get some breakfast, analyze the day and work to make it productive and profitable."

I'd also noticed on Day 1 the rep was struggling with objections. He'd fold with each objection and even agreed with the customer at times when it really wasn't appropriate or necessary. So over breakfast, we reviewed accounts, broke them down to follow-ups that could be handled by phone, and identified which targets might actually buy something. Once we'd done that, we worked to anticipate potential objections. "Let's practice overcoming these objections," I instructed.

Yep, the dreaded role-play. Love it or hate it, it works. Reps are able to practice their delivery, including body posture, tonality, pace of speech, staying on message, inflection, staying within a prescribed time windows, etc. The more the role-play, the more they become comfortable with the proper cadence of the call, and specific language that triggers a desire to purchase.

I'd also assumed [note: assumed] my new sales team had been calling on qualified/strategic customers. I had no doubt they were well-trained on product knowledge, sales process, overcoming objections and being efficient with their time and sales pitch.

I could never have been more wrong ... seriously.

It was time for a serious course-correction.

I asked each of my salespeople to rethink their business plans [assuming they had ever even had done one]. I also created a Business Plan Template they could complete, including:

- A list of all their accounts, sorted largest-to-smallest.

- Assigning mini-territories within their overall territory [6-8 accounts per territory, leading to greater efficiencies and reducing unnecessary "windshield time'].

- A list of specific "fill the hole" items for each targeted account.

- A list of their 25 largest opportunities, ranked from highest-to-lowest.

With this in place, prior to traveling with them, I would send them an email letting them know I would like to work in mini-territory 1 and 2, for example. I would give them two weeks' notice, so they could plan and set appointments.

I'd also tell them that I wanted to call on the largest opportunities. I would single out key accounts I wanted to see and identify specific products I wanted them to emphasize. Further, I asked them to anticipate potential objections and start preparing for how to handle these. We would discuss these by phone a few days before my visit.

I wasn't trying to be a brutal taskmaster, I simply wanted each one of my reps to succeed, and for our team to be among the best, if not the best. Admittedly, this is *a lot of work* for the sales manager! This level of preparation takes time, but is critical for success.

In my opinion, based on years of experience in the trenches and *overseeing* the trenches, pre-call planning is HUGE for Sales Managers and their reps. I strongly believe 40% of your time should be spent planning, 40% spent in the field and 20% on "all other stuff".

After I developed and implemented the business plan template and worked with reps to create a winner, my field visits *doubled* in productivity. Our breakfast meetings became more like batting practice, taking a few more warm-up swings before the game began. My sales reps also began gaining more confidence and, in turn, closing more business. That's why I like the John Wooden quote at the head of this chapter.

Bottom line: *It is in practice where the real teaching begins.*

Pre-work was critical, but equally as critical is follow-up. Either that evening or the next day at the latest, as Sales Manager, I would follow up with the rep on the two days of sales calls just completed.

In this follow-up, I used what I called a "sandwich correspondence" approach. As you know, making a sandwich starts with a single piece of bread, then the meat, cheese, tomato and then another piece of bread.

- Paragraph 1: Start with a thank you for the rep's time and remind them of the positive aspects of our day.

- Paragraph 2: Here you identify key follow-up activities needed, things to work on and how you can help them. That's the meat.

- Paragraph 3: Reconfirm your faith in them being able to obtain their goal/quota and remind them you are on their side. That's the second slice of bread.

Start positive, give constructive feedback and finish with a "You are great!"-type of encouragement and a call-to-action such as "Go get 'em!"

Of course, if a rep is a low performer, it's a altogether different communication which has to be handled delicately but firmly and customized to the rep's shortcoming and areas for improvement. Also, it's good to include their numbers are performing versus sales quota and sales of strategic products. They'll quickly note the fact they're lagging behind and need to "up their game" to succeed and grow within the organization.

In summary:

- Set expectations for the field sales visit

- Schedule a breakfast meeting and take some pre-game "batting practice"

- Coach as you go [in between calls]

- Follow up on a timely basis with "sandwich-style" correspondence, including action steps

When working with multiple salespeople, it's important to see yourselves as a team; a single unit consisting of multiple players whose individual preparation and game-time execution benefits them individually and the team at-large.

Also, be proactive! Don't just wait for something to develop or hope that things will improve.

For example, if your tennis partner is at the net and the opponent hits a great lob, *you* need to go after it. Don't just stand there, be active. Help when and where you can.

The best Sales Managers know their products and how to sell them as well, or even better, than their reps. A Sales Manager who doesn't bring anything to the table on sales calls is just taking up space and wasting the company's money. Bring something to the table. Your sales reps will love you for it and they'll know you truly *do* have their backs.

"To everything there is a season..." – Ecclesiastes 3:1

CHAPTER 8

THE LIFE CYCLE OF A SALES REPRESENTATIVE

As Sales Manager, you can expect your sales people to fall into one of four stages along what I call "the life cycle of a sales representative". Similar to the life cycle of a product, sales representatives evolve and grow and typically begin to decline as time marches on ... and it always does. The stages are:

1. EARLY LEARNING

2. RAPID GROWTH

3. MATURITY

4. DECLINING

I developed this theory over a period of seven years when I was focused on accelerating the sales growth of new sales representatives. I studied, compared and made notes about how different salespeople [with varying levels of experience] performed at different stages of the life cycle.

Let's take a closer look ...

EARLY LEARNING STAGE – These are folks you've just hired. Could be a total greenhorn with little or no experience or someone still trying to establish themselves in the world of sales with only a few years under their belt.

Without a doubt, the most important time with new-hires is the first 30 days. This includes onboarding, training and finding the right POSITIVE mentor from the beginning. Obviously, you need to stay close to new-hires and be an active participant in their development for them to grow and prosper [and make you look like you're a star Master Class instructor].

Assigning the right mentor is CRITICAL! If you are a small organization, then it needs to be you as Sales Manager. If you do not have the desire to teach then it's incumbent upon you to find someone who has that desire and assign them to the new sales rep.

So, what does a mentor do?

- First and foremost, they must be **a positive, genuine ambassador** for your company. They need to not only nurture the rookie but reinforce the great decision they made when joining your company.
- They need to be **highly competent**. Too many times, I observed "trainers" with sub-par attitudes or who were average at best in sales training and product knowledge. No one believes you want to train someone to be average so make sure you've got one of your high-achievers tethered to the newbie.

Being highly competent means they know the company's products, how to position them, and how to outduel competition. The best sales trainers I've seen truly enjoyed teaching and guiding others. Their delivery was upbeat and positive, they were great company ambassadors, had high morals and ethics, and were outstanding sales professionals with an established track record of sustained success.

Their "secret ingredient" might be their ability to ask probing questions, their product knowledge, or their demonstration skills [or all of the above]. I also found most trainers were extremely likable which probably played a large part in their career advancement.

While being highly competent is very, very important, I also believe a positive attitude is even more important. I say this because you can have a trainer who knows their "stuff" inside and out, but their attitude and delivery come across as negative. They use phrases like "Let me give you the real scoop around here" or they gossip about other team members and, worst of all, are passive-aggressive. Who needs that …?

A good way to solve the trainer competency issue is to create an excellent training manual. A person may have great potential to be a trainer but if they're not equipped with the right information, their guidance will miss the mark.

History's greatest sailors never left port without an established destination and a charted course; incorporating variables such as wind, weather, currents, sea depths, vessel traffic, safety plans, etc., etc., etc. And they course-corrected along the way.

In actuality, charting your own course and creating an excellent sales manual isn't that difficult. It simply takes time, insight and knowledge. Be sure to incorporate:

1. **Your Company's Story** – How was it formed and why? What inspired its founder[s]? What are its historical milestones, the good being done in the community, and anything that pertains to helping your customers and your customers' customers. The more detail and the more "points of pride", the better. Other key items to cover are manufacturing processes [noting products made in the USA], hiring initiatives [i.e., veterans' special needs, minorities, etc.], emphasis on using environmentally safe production materials and processes, etc.

2. **Policies and Procedures** – HR guidelines, compensation plan, allowable expenses and filing procedures, Paid Time Off, healthcare and

investment benefits, and Code of Conduct [If you do not have a Code of Conduct, create one. Trust me, it will be needed from time to time.]

3. **Internal Contacts** – Answer the trainee's question, "Whom do I call for ...?" Create and update a roster with all employee names, roles, email address and cell numbers. You might even include personal touches such as birthdays, spouse's name and children's names, hobbies, special interests, community involvement, etc. [Check with HR before adding the personal info to ensure you're aligned with your company's privacy policies.]

Also, everyone in the company should be made aware of the new-hire and asked to reach out and welcome them, ideally face-to-face. Sharing business cards, whether it's done hand-to-hand or digitally, is helpful, too.

4. **Internal Reports** – Include sales tracking templates [weekly, monthly, quarterly, annually] to record and review business activity and results. This also a great tool – a "report card" of sorts -- for identifying strengths and weaknesses and to identify where additional coaching or instruction might be helpful. Share a few examples of well-executed sales reports.

5. **Key Reference Info at Their Fingertips** – Pre-loaded onto laptops and/or tablets, incorporating essential information, guidelines and FAQs.

6. **EZ/Quick Reference Items** – "Cheat sheet" of selling Skills Basics.

7. **Product Literature** – Include product design, features and benefits, and other info, advantages versus competitive products [validated with solid data].

8. **A List of Probing Questions** – Queries for your customer or potential customer to learn more about their needs, challenges, etc.

9. **A 90-Day Plan** – Include targets [categorized by highest profit potential, most likely to buy, and long-term targets] sales deadlines, planned tactics, etc.

10. **Strategic Business Plan Template.** – The easier you make it to "fill in the blanks", the more likely it is someone will put pen to paper or fingers to keyboard or tablet. Formalizing the Strategic Business Plan is an excellent exercise in focus and a convenient tool to reference when needed. It's a great idea for sales reps to start each day by quickly reviewing their plan, thereby refreshing their memory and sharpening their focus on priorities.

11. **Special Perks** – Ideally, there are some perks available to you at your company such as discounts on company products, discounts from vendors/associated vendors, etc.

Trainers also need to be reasonably accessible and always approachable. The worst thing you can do is assign a mentor to someone and they disappear after initial training [typically the stage when new-hires have the most questions and need the most guidance]. Ironically this often happens due to a trainer being very good at what they do, and therefore very busy and in-demand. You can solve this by compensating them incrementally for their time. Pay a trainer a bonus for taking new reps under their seasoned and skilled wings.

RAPID GROWTH STAGE – This is the stage when a rep is most likely to be at their best in terms of performance, productivity and profit generated. Typically occurring after 2-3 years, the Rapid Growth Stage is when a rep has been well-trained, has mastered the product line, knows his or her customers very well, and is up to the challenges of selling successfully against competition.

In order to keep this group on fire, you must do five critical things:

1. Provide them with any and all resources and support your company might have to help them accelerate sales. For example, increase

promotional monies, provide them more product samples, or give them the latest tablet or cellphone with exciting new apps pre-loaded. If they ask for additional strategic sales training or other relevant training to be more productive, by all means, make it happen. Leveraging their desire to excel benefits everyone. Offer to reimburse their expenses related to gaining a Master's degree but do this with the caveat they stay with the company for an established period of time after completing their studies. If opportunity knocks elsewhere and they move on, use a sliding scale for reimbursement.

2. Increase their compensation. Not necessarily base salary but higher commissions once they hit established benchmarks. High-achievers deserve to be the highest paid members of your sales team.

3. Involve them in your company's strategic/tactical plans. Seek their counsel on what they believe is needed to grow the business, and grow it faster. A seat at The Big Table is important to sales people and makes them feel valued and appreciated.

4. Recognize them. Give them awards, gift cards, trips for great performance. Compliment them in front of peers and colleagues. Send them encouraging emails and/or texts and let them know you appreciate their hard work and dedication.

5. If they truly are superstars and *outstanding* at what they do, a shot at an equity share in the company would be a phenomenal incentive. Save this option for the elite-of-the-elite.

You must also understand and accept this is the stage when reps are most likely to leave your company for better pay or perceived sexier jobs. Also, decades of studies consistently show people don't quit companies, they quit bosses. Make sure you have goggles on the most talented and highest-performing individuals. Be sure they're being managed but not over-managed.

Do anything within reason to stoke their loyalty and commitment to your company, your products, and your team. Nobody wants to lose a superstar or a budding superstar to free agency, especially to the competition.

MATURITY STAGE -- In this stage, you have a rep that's been around for five years or more. They are now well-versed on your products and have strong relationships with their best customers [though this can vary based on competency and industriousness].

Their previously hard-charging, high-energy efforts are more refined and polished. They have a palpable sense of quiet confidence and grace as they go about selling, and are able to quickly earn and maintain the respect and trust of customers and prospects [and peers, for that matter]. People have faith in them and know they're reliable. Their numbers ...? Well, they speak for themselves.

During this stage, these folks often attract interest from other companies. And they're likely entertaining new offers simply because they've become bored with their success and want to move along. Believe it or not, it happens. A lot. Sales people are by nature restless and desire new challenges to keep them engaged, energized and motivated.

[In today's world, it seems younger people in general, and younger sales reps in particular, reach the "I'm bored" stage faster. More than ever before, there's a desire for instant gratification so the Maturity Stage may actually be a dying breed.]

Keep an eye on those you believe to be either approaching or in the Maturity Stage. Think about it: You have a well-trained person who knows their territory and customers, they have a great track record, and their career is on an upward trajectory. These people are your most efficient weapons in growing your business. So, what should you do if you sense they may soon be leaving?

If they make reasonable requests for higher base pay, an improved commission structure, more PTO, or other "bennies", find a way to grant them their wish. If the demands are beyond your reach right now, stall their departure as long as possible. Something may suddenly become an option that isn't available today. Ask them to be patient a bit longer. If they do decide to leave, wish them well ... and stay in touch! Sometimes people discover the grass isn't always greener on the other side.

If you find yourself with reps in the Maturity Stage, you must understand, no matter how good they are, they *also* need your attention and motivation. Don't fall for the line, "I'm good. I don't need help. Go spend time with the newer folks." When you're an established high-performer, it's hard for them to admit they could use a little coddling or a pep talk.

Folks in this stage typically *are* good at new product introductions because they know their customer base and can approach friendly customers early to pre-sell. What I find, having managed in many different divisions, is that if you're not launching new products, reps often lose interest and can become disgruntled. If your new-product pipeline is currently empty, it may be a good idea to give them additional territory. New hunting ground can re-energize a mature rep.

Also, these folks would benefit from having you, as Sales Manager, arranging for members of your company's senior management team to meet their largest customers. This deepens the already positive relationship you enjoy with your customer. Because they've been good customers for a while, introducing them to your senior leadership helps validate their decision to do business with you ... and *not* "the other guy".

Another thing you can do to keep reps engaged is to put them on a project that stretches their capabilities. Expose them to priority marketing or operational activities. Include them in important business planning and strategy activities.

In one of the divisions I worked in, we researched why Mature Stage sales reps left the company. Studying a five-year period, we found that 40% of this group left due to the company outlook being poor. They felt their ability to win was less than what it would be at one of our competitors. Others felt we weren't launching enough products or launching "the right ones."

Twenty percent left due to burnout or lifestyle, tired of chasing increasingly demanding quotas year after year after year. Paradoxically, success in sales can seem punitive at times. One minute you're onstage receiving a handsome plaque and a healthy check along with gushing words of praise. The next minute you get your quota for the upcoming year and you feel like your just-rewarded efforts and success are no longer good enough. In truth, they're not. That's the nature of sales. Some would say, "No rest for the weary" while others will tell you if you don't comply, it's "Next man [or woman] up!"

That's why many leave to pursue a similar job at a new company where the demands aren't quite as stringent, or they choose to embark on an altogether new career. It takes someone special to be able to endure the demands of a sales position.

We also found 20% left the division due to promotion. And another 20% left for higher pay and commissions. A handful of reps left for a variety of reasons in other categories [i.e., retirement, family demands, a desire to take an extended period of time away from the workplace, etc.].

After analyzing the results of the study, we decided to focus on the group that believed our business outlook was lacking. One way to attack this was to get them more deeply involved in business planning, as well as creating a Senior Sales Council where they could voice issues and concerns early and often.

An effective sales council is more than just a place to vent your frustrations or complain about matters. It needs to be a safe zone where reps and managers can bring to the table what they believe to be barriers to growth along with insights and possible solutions. Members should be a sounding board *and* a voice for the field sales team.

DECLINING STAGE -- In this stage, similar to a product's life cycle, it's time to divest. In other words, it's time to part ways. The signs of a disengaged sales rep are pretty clear:

- They become less and less visible.

- They start withdrawing.

- Customer and colleague complaints about them increase.

- Their once-timely and accurate reports and communication are poor.

- They become increasingly negative about, pretty much, everything.

You get the picture. It should never get to this point but, unfortunately, many sales people retire *while still on the job!*

In sales, it's easy to hide. Everyone gets busy doing this and that and for a salesperson, it's easy to just stay home and watch TV, surf the internet, play golf with friends, or sleep in. If they have a decent book of business, sometimes you won't notice their decline in performance for months. It's up to you to detect this early and put a plan in place to either course-correct or bid them adieu.

A while back, I saw a book entitled *Don't Fire Them: Fire Them Up!* I didn't actually read the book but I loved the title and the concept. Six words said it all.

We all know how expensive it is to hire a new person. Sometimes it can be expensive to *fire* a person, too, if they believe the decision to terminate was inappropriate and a court has to decide or a legal settlement has to be paid.

Turnover can cost you 6-9 months of an individual's salary, not to mention lost sales and sales opportunities, as well as opening the door to competition to come in and administer a double-whammy: You not only lose the account, you lose it to your primary competitor. Ouch.

Wouldn't it be better to have a plan in place so your sales reps never reach the Declining Stage? *Absolutely!*

Having said that, if you have such a rep, it's on you to assess whether or not this individual is worth saving. Unfortunately, when things get to the Declining Stage, the likelihood of a successful reclamation project is overwhelmingly rare. Many times, cutting ties is best for all.

Also, don't assume this stage only affects reps with 5+ years on the job. A salesperson's performance can begin to decline within a year or two. [If it were a medical condition, it would be called Early Onset Malaise.]

They may have decided the job was not for them and checked out mentally. Or they've simply lost interest and the desire to excel. In sales, people tend to stay on until they find something better which can take a few months or a couple of years. You definitely want to avoid having someone on the payroll who has one foot in the door and the other out [or even worse, inside your competitor's door].

In summary:

- Assign the RIGHT MENTOR for the EARLY LEARNING STAGE.

- **FEED THE MONSTER** with resources at the **RAPID GROWTH STAGE.**

- Find a **NEW HUNTING GROUND** at the **MATURITY STAGE.**

- **SAY GOODBYE** at the **DECLINING STAGE.**

You can only successfully navigate the life cycle of a sales rep by being an active, ongoing participant in the development of your entire sales team.

One final thought ...

In my 30 years in the corporate world, I noticed far too often the sales organization was blamed when profits were down. It's easy to point fingers at reps ... when the finger should actually be pointed at the Sales Manager in the mirror.

Be proactive and constantly assess your strategy. See yourself as a mariner and course-correct when necessary and do it quickly to get back on track. Reps may be doing everything you've asked them to do but if you've charted an inaccurate course, you'll never arrive at your intended destination. Rework your strategy to get back on target.

Something to think about.

CONCLUSION

When I set out to write this book and share any sales-related wisdom and knowledge I might've gleaned over three decades in the corporate world, I did so knowing I couldn't possibly tell you everything there is to know about selling.

That's because the selling process is a living, breathing, ever-evolving entity and some of what works today may not work down the road. And down the road, undoubtedly, will be all-new sales tactics and practices that don't even exist today. That's why it's so important to attack your sales career with an always-open mind and an eagerness to learn and improve. Even the absolute best salesperson can learn new tricks.

One thing that will *never* change is the fact that selling is *absolutely the lifeblood* of any organization. Building and nurturing a robust sales organization should be the No.1 priority of every CEO.

Period. End of debate.

As I mentioned early in this little book of mine, I will never forget a critical business planning meeting I attended while working at Johnson & Johnson. The company flew in the best and the brightest in our organization in hopes of developing breakthrough strategies and ideas to achieve exponential growth. Exciting stuff!

More than 100 of the most talented individuals in our company, many holding Ivy League MBAs and identified as High Potentials, gathered to do our best collective brainstorming. The cost of this meeting was easily more than $250,000.

We broke into groups with a top consulting company serving as facilitator. Each group holed up in a breakout room for two days and was expected to make a formal presentation of our best thinking to the Management Board. The goal: Create a blockbuster, out-of-the-box plan or strategy to *double our business* in five years.

[Note some of the words I just used: *best and brightest, exponential growth, breakthrough, blockbuster*, and *out-of-the-box*? That was our mission.]

As the business planning meeting drew to a close and after all group presentations were made, the Management Board determined the presentation entitled *Doing the Basics Better* was the winner. It specified the need for better sales training, tools, techniques, etc. to improve our basic blocking and tackling. After two days of brain-draining, hard work, I shook my head and thought, "Wow, we spent all this time, money and brainpower, and *this* is the winner ..?"

Well, it wasn't until I spent another 10 years with the company, serving in many different roles, that I realized doing the basics better truly *is* the key to success! [And BTW, we didn't actually double our business simply because it was an overly ambitious goal against an unrealistic deadline. We did, however, bone up on the fundamentals and post solid growth over the next five years.]

Aside from hitting the occasional grand slam on a new product or service, it's the everyday fundamentals, done well, that determines who succeeds ... and who doesn't. It's true in every sport, every company, every organization that sets goals and seeks to achieve. If doing the basics better isn't a priority, you're spinning your wheels.

Don't spin your wheels!

Build a sales team of the best blockers and tacklers you can find, emphasize the importance of fundamentals, and coach 'em up early and often.

I wish you every success. *Now go get 'em!*

REACH OUT

To contact the author:

- **eMail:** mirstrategicsolutions@gmail.com

- **Cell:** 954.256.4350

Learn more about Joe Mir at www.linkedin.com/in/joemir

ABOUT THE AUTHOR

Joe currently serves as a consultant in the healthcare industry based in Weston, FL. He has more than three decades of experience working in the medical devices industry, including positions in sales, sales management, marketing, international business, and national accounts. He has negotiated and executed numerous contracts with regional Group Purchasing Organizations and Integrated Delivery Networks throughout the country. He has extensive experience developing relationships with senior leaders and key clinical personnel at health systems.

Prior to becoming a consultant, Joe spent 25 years at Johnson & Johnson in a variety of roles. He was a member of the VP of Sales and Global Marketing Council as well as a Board Member. Joe started as an orthopedic sales representative in Florida and after two years was promoted to Western Regional Sales Manager for the U.S. West Coast, where he won consecutive Regional Manager of the Year awards. Joe then moved into a marketing role for Ethicon, a division of Johnson & Johnson, in Latin America and was promoted to Director of Marketing for Latin America and was recognized in the Johnson & Johnson Annual Report for launching new technologies in developing countries.

Joe returned to corporate sales/strategic accounts in spine, orthopedics, trauma, and sports medicine and achieved 4 area of the year awards. He was one of five people selected nationally to negotiate innovative contracting for all DePuy franchises in the Southeast [$1 billion business]. As Director of Strategic Accounts, he led the first signing of a major orthopedic service line contract for DePuy Synthes.

Joe earned a Bachelor of Business Administration degree from the University of Miami in Florida and has a Healthcare Certificate from the Wharton School of Business. He is a Board Member at Friends of South Florida Autism, which serves the children who are most severely affected with autism.